14.95

Libretto

Edoardo Sanguineti

translated from the Italian by

Pádraig J. Daly

Poetry Europe Series No. 5

The Dedalus Press
24 The Heath
Cypress Downs
Dublin 6W
Ireland

ISBN 1 901233 20 0

Cover painting by **Ciarán Lennon**

Dedalus Press books are distributed in the U.K. by
Central Books, Ltd. 99 Wallis Road, London E9 5LN,
and in the U.S.A. and Canada by
Dufour Editions Inc., PO Box 7, Chester Springs,
Pennsylvania 19425 – 0007

The Dedalus Press receives financial assistance from An
Chomhairle Ealaíon, The Arts Council, Ireland

Printed by Colour Books Ltd., Dublin

PREFACE

Edoardo Sanguineti was born in Genoa in 1930. He is professor of Italian Literature in his native city. His work is very highly regarded in Italy and he gives readings all over the world yet most of his poetry remains untranslated into English. This book is a translation of the whole of his 1995 booklet, "Libretto".

Critics have loved to describe Sanguineti in the context of movements and schools. This does not interest me. I am attracted to his work because of the marvellous fun he has with words. He draws words from umpteen languages and myriad areas of experience and scholarship. He plays with them, teases with them, puts them congruously and incongruously up against one another. And they lead him down all kinds of side roads and passageways; but never in a way that fails to illuminate or runs out of the control of his extraordinary intellect.

Sanguineti's work is ongoing, like that of Thomas Kinsella in Ireland, building slowly into an impressive oeuvre. At the end of each piece by Sanguineti there is no full stop, merely a colon; we are invited forward, to the next poem, to the next book.

Translating the work of so formidable a word ludist, such a trawler of language and languages, is a crazy task. "Similtriboulet", for instance. I tried several dictionaries for it before a friend explained to me that "triboulet" is French for, among other things, "a mandrel, a miner's pick, a ring guage, a wooden cylinder used by goldsmiths for rounding articles, a tragic buffoon". (Dineen, eat your heart out!)

Then there was "Quaqua". Was it a duck's call or were we dealing with the Latin for "Wheresoever"?

And what was to be done with puns and jokes and the juxtapositioning of words like "Mortalmente" with "Moralmente". Often I had to admit defeat and work out some inadequate compromise.

So why bother to translate at all?

Because Sanguineti's book, when I came across it, excited me. And on the "Bonum est duffusivum sui" principle, I needed people to know.

Because Sanguineti is so fascinating a man, expressing beneath all his learned wordplay a beautiful, sad romantic sensibility. Look no further than the poem about the acrobat which opens this book: "cosi mi ruoto e salto, io nel tuo cuore".

Because his poetry is so life-affirming. Look for instance at the third poem and its resounding conclusion: "me la sono goduta, io, la mia vita". Look anywhere.

Because even the poorest translation may lead people to read more of him. And after all, Japanese, Estonians and Greeks can read and enjoy, with whatever losses, versions of Joyce's "Ulysses", in their own languages. Sanguineti likewise deserves to be enjoyed by a public, until now sadly lacking, beyond the confines of his native tongue, in the wide world of English monoglotism. Maybe this work will inspire others to introduce English readers to a wider range of his writing.

The failures in these translations are entirely my own. Much that is good in them is owed to John Barnes and John F. Deane who read the first drafts and offered many valuable suggestions and corrections. Thanks, too, to my friend Nicole Arnould, for whom even similtriboulets are unproblematic.

Pádraig J. Daly, September 1998

I

acrobata (s.m.) è chi cammina tutto in punta (di piedi): (tale, almeno,
è per l'etimo): poi procede, però, naturalmente, tutto in punta di dita, anche,
di mani (e in punta di forchetta): e sopra la sua testa: (e sopra i chiodi,
fachireggiando e funamboleggiando): (e sopra i fili tesi tra due case, per le strade
e le piazze: dentro un trapezio, in un circo, in un cerchio, sopra un cielo):
volteggia su due canne, flessibilmente, infilzate in due bicchieri, in due scarpe,
in due guanti: (dentro il fumo, nell'aria): pneumatico e somatico, dentro il vuoto
pneumatico: (dentro pneumatici plastici, dentro botti e bottiglie): e salta mortalmente:
e mortalmente (e moralmente) ruota:

(così mi ruoto e salto, io nel tuo cuore):

I

an acrobat (n. masc.) is one who walks all on a point (on tiptoe): (that, at least, is
the etymology): then proceeds, mark you, effortlessly, totally on fingertips, and,
on the tips of his hands (and on a fork's tip): on his head (and on nails
fakiring and funambuling): (and on tightropes stretched between two houses, on streets
and piazzas: on a trapeze, in a circus, in a circle, on a sky):
he circles, lithely, on two sticks, stuck into two beakers, into two shoes,
into two gloves: (inside the smoke, within the air): pneumatic and somatic, inside pneumatic
emptiness: (inside plastic pneumatic tyres, in barrels and bottles): and he somersaults perilously:
and periously (and ethically) spins:

(so do I spin and somersault in your heart):

II

che cosa ti chiedo, se chiedi, ti crittorispondo così:

un microU (una specie
di similtriboulet, storto i suoi arti corti) si fa innanzi dondoloso,
ghignando malizioso, scortato da un armato luminoso: (con T gli fa chiarura,
in quella scena oscura): (e tarda è l'ora, come risulta ancora da un quadrante
gigante di un orologio mogio di un torrione di un palazzaccio diaccio,
siglato M): (che indica, a piacere, un gruppetto di numeri romani, rotanti
tra l'I e il XII): siamo, come si dice, pressappoco, à quatre heures du matin:
(nel pieno di un'estate festaiuola):

questa è la mia richiesta: e adesso vedi tu
(e dico tu che sai): insomma, noi vedremo (se vedremo): (io vedrò, tu vedrai):

II

if you want to know what I want of you, I'll answer cryptically thus:

a microU (a kind of
similtriboulet, its short limbs distorted) comes advancing unsteadily,
sneering maliciously, escorted by a shining guard: (with T there's added clarity
to that dark scene): (and the hour is late, as we can observe from the huge
dial of a crestfallen clock on the turret of a great palace of ice, chilly
marked M): (which shows, as it pleases, a cluster of roman numerals, circling
from I to XII): we are, so to speak, near enough à quatre heures du matin:
(at the height of a festive summer):

that is my request: so now consider it
(I mean you who understand): to summarise, we shall see (if we shall see): (I shall see, you shall see):

III

incidetele a lettere di scatola, miei lettori testamentari (e parlo ai miei scolari,
gli ipocriti miei figli, i filoproletari che tanto mi assomigliano, innumerevoli,
ormai, come i grani di sabbia del vacuo mio deserto), queste parole mie, sopra la tomba
mia, con la saliva, intingendovi un dito nella bocca: (come io lo intingo, adesso,
tra gli eccessivi ascessi delle algide mie gengive):

                    me la sono goduta, io, la mia vita:

III

carve in huge letters, you readers of my will (and I speak to my pupils,
my hypocrite children, the lovers of the proletariat who are so like me, numberless,
by now, as the grains of sand in my empty desert), over my grave, these words of mine,
with spit, dipping a finger in your mouths: (as I now dip my finger
in amidst the excessive abcesses of my frozen gums):

I have truly enjoyed my life:

IV

è questa l'esca fresca, in questi versi, che infilzo alla mia floscia R moscia,
quasi fosse un rugoso profilattico tattico, bitorzoloso e galattico:

(e il papi
l'ho scannato, la mami l'ho chiavata): (ho fatto i miei progressi, lento lento,
a quattro zampe, e poi a due, e a tre):

tutti i lucchetti ho sciolto (non esclusi
gli indovinalagrillo, le sciarade incatenate, i logogrifi, i palindromi): (e
questo stesso rebus, che ti scrivo):

(sono il tuo tu, sono il tuo TA, mia sfinge):

IV

in these verses, notice the fresh bait I skewer onto my limp guttural R,
as if it were a tactical wrinkled prophylactic, knotty and galactic:

                                                                    and I have slaughtered
the papilla and screwed the mamilla): (I have made my progress, bit by bit,
on four paws, then on two, then on three):

                    I have released all the locks (not excluding
the conundrums, the tethered charades, the wordpuzzles, the palindromes): (and
this very riddle, which I write to you):

                    (I am your own you, I am your TA, my sphinx):

v

con gli occhi caldi, qui, del dottor Spensley (se metto insieme e preistoria
e protostoria e storia), un secolo calcistico mi scruta: (sta mezzo abbandonato,
le gambe accavallate: trascura un volumone, aperto lì al suo fianco, per guardarmi,
e tutti gli altri libri, schierati là negli scaffali, fitti: e si regge la testa,
con una mano, taciturno, ormai):

la vecchia sfera gira sempre, tra i nostri piedi,
inquieta, accarezzata dai venti marini: (e, sotto i nostri piedi, ruota ancora
la sfera del pianeta):

fotografie superstiti (piene di tempo, popolate di morti
noti e ignoti) additano, per frammenti di lampi, questa lunga leggenda:

è rossa, è blu:

V

here with the warm eyes of doctor Spensley (I'm putting prehistory, protohistory
and history together), a footballing century scrutinizes me: (it is waiflike
and crosslegged: keeps ignoring the huge book lying open beside it, to look at me,
and all the other books, ranged densely on the shelves: and it holds up its head
with one hand, taciturnly):

      the ancient ball rolls continually between our feet,
restless, caressed by sea breezes: (and, under our feet, the round ball of the world
still turns):

    surviving photographs (filled up with time, peopled by the dead,
known and unknown) illumine this long tale with lightning flashes:

      it is red, it is blue:

VI

se mi stacco da te, mi strappo tutto:

ma il mio meglio (o il mio peggio)
ti rimane attaccato, appiccicoso, come un miele, una colla, un olio denso:
ritorno in me, quando ritorno in te: (e mi ritrovo i pollici e i polmoni):
tra poco atterro a Madrid:

(in coda qui all'aereo, selezionati miei connazionali,
gente d'affari, dicono numeri e numeri, mentre bevono e fumano, eccitati,
agitatamente ridendo):

vivo ancora per te, se vivo ancora:

VI

if I splice myself from you, I slice myself apart:

    but the best of me (or the worst)

still clings to you, stickily, like honey, like glue, like a thick oil:
I come back to myself when I come back to you: (and I recover my thumbs and my lungs):
in a while I'll alight in Madrid:

                    (ranged behind me on the plane, a sampling of fellow Italians,
businesspeople, totting and totting up numbers, while drinking and smoking, excited,
laughing nervously):

            I live still for you, if still I'm alive:

VII

eccomi qua, moscone che delira doloroso, risibile, ostensibile, che ronza
recluso dentro un solido bicchiere: (c'è una goccia di vino, manca l'aria):
da questa residencia non si evade: (o si evade, nuotando, dentro un tasso
inimmaginabile di umidità, impensabile in maggio): per un qualunque soprabito,
potrei donare Castiglia e Aragona:

ma per averti, per sentirti e toccarti,
con le mie zampe fragili e pelose, non mi basta di svendere, nemmeno, l'immensa
totalità dei miei occhi, che moltiplica, appena, una prigione:

(ho conosciuto,
adesso, uno zoologo sivigliano, ricercatore in pensione, che zoppica una gamba
rigidissima): (sta con la moglie, però si dispera):

ci è bloccato il telefono, persino:

VII

look! here I am, I'm a bluebottle, frenziedly, mournfully, ludicrously, visibly, buzzing
prisoned in a sturdy tumbler: (there's a wee drop of wine, but little air):
from this residencia there's no hope of escape: (or if I do, I'll flounder in unimaginable
levels of humidity, inconceivable in May): for some kind of overcoat,
I'd give Castille and Aragon:

               but to have you, to feel you and touch you,
with my fragile and furry paws, I'd gladly exchange, and more, the vast
totality my eyes take in, which a prison, scarcely, increases:

                              (just now I have met
a Sevillian zoologist, a retired researcher, who hobbles along on the stiffest
of legs): (he is living with his wife, but despairs):

                           now even our telephone's cut off:

VIII

dentro il cattivo retiro, tra le bancarelle della fiera (un ballerino giallo e verde
e bianco sfidava il fango, fiacco, piroettando), sprofondammo prima in tre, poi
in quattro: (la scoperta delle architetture cartacee, da sforbiciarsi con disperata
tenacia tutta iberica, e delle molli frittelle, da ingurgitarsi inzuppate,
avvenne poco dopo, con le lacustri e tacite quaquà, che sono universali,
invece):

    ma è molto tardi, è notte buia, e già chiudono tutto, e arriva il taxi:

VIII

in this awful retiro, amid the fairground booths (a yellow and green and white
balleerino defied the mud, wearily pirouetting), we collapsed, three to begin with,
then the four of us: (the discovery of the cardboard architecture, to be cut out with desperate
absolutely Iberian tenacity, and of the soft pancakes, to be gobbled up still soaked,
came a little later, together with those silent lacustrine wheresoevers which, on the other hand,
can everywhere be found):

but it is very late, it is dark night, already everything is closing down,
the taxi is here:

IX

tutto sommato (scrisse), l'esistente, in generale (siamo nel '26:
siamo nel mese di aprile), è una modesta imperfezione:

(modesta,
certo, a paragone dell'immenso non esistente, del puro e semplice
niente): è un'irregolarità, una mostruosità:

la voce mia, così, la mia
scrittura, orribilmente deturpano, lo so (per poco, ancora), la suprema
armonia dell'agrafia, dell'afasia:

(già rinuncio, dislessico, a rileggermi):

IX

all told (he wrote), existence, taking it in general (this is '26:
the month is April), is a slight imperfection:

(slight

indeed, when you compare it to the immense non-existence, to pure and simple
nothingness): it's an irregularity, a monstrosity:

my voice, then, my

writing, horridly distort, I know (for a wee while yet), the supreme
harmony of agraphia, of aphasia:

(already, dyslexic, I refuse to re-read myself):

sabato sera, andando solo solo unter den Linden, lì all'altezza, all'incirca,
di una sopravvissuta Liebknechtbrücke (era il deserto, nel giardino, intorno
ai due poveri classici), vidi, di colpo, le Hypernynfomani Hyponynfette
(un duecento, diciamo, un due e cinquanta), che marciavano, streghine svelte,
in scortato corteo scordato (e strillavano amore, si capisce, per i Take That,
dentro un vuoto on the rocks di un vento roco):

si alzò però, solido e secco, allora, uno scomposto coro di pubescenti Lumpenominidi:
(non sto a doppiarti le parole e i gesti: ma ti indovini avambracci e pugnacci,
e bassissimi ventri all'elvispelvis, come ai perduti tempi del Love Me Tender
e di altre morte teddyrockettate, di quel tono e quel tipo):

sull'altro marciapiede, megafonico,

e diceva,

quel disperato messaggio geloso, se mixi bene gli ululati e le mimiche:
ci stiamo noi, per voi, puttane nane, se è soltanto che girate, da queste parti
qui, con la voglia di farvi un po' infilare, non si sa mai, sveltamente, nel caso:

X

Saturday evening, walking all all alone unter den Linden, there at approximately the level
of a surviving Liebknechtbrücke (it was a wilderness, in the garden, around the
two classical wretches,) I saw, of a sudden, the Hypernymphomaniac Hyponymphettes
(about two hundred, let's say, or two fifty), who were marching, the sprightly hags,
escorted in a discordant procession (screaming out their love, I'll have you know, for Take That,
inside an on the rocks void of a hoarse wind):

on the other footpath, megaphonically,
there rose then, sharply and firmly, a dishevelled chorus of pubescent Lumpenhominids:
(I won't repeat their words and gestures: but you can imagine their forearms and fists,
and low-slung bellies like Elvispelvis, in those lost times of Love Me Tender
and other defunct teddyrockerisms, of that same type and tone):

and that
desperate envious message said, if you mix correctly their ululations and gesticulations:
here we are then, all yours, you midget harlots, if you're only wandering about, right here,
with the desire to have yourselves entered, you never know, hurriedly, in the off-chance:

la più graziosa grazia (e più efficace) è la ragazza che mi aggancia in Tegel,
acquattata in agguato, per caricarmi sopra un fuoristrada, per scaricarmi a un Hilton
(Kroneflügel): poi l'ho mancata al telefono (e per quell'Empfang, là al Beethoven-Saal,
con l'orazione della borgomastra, mi era quasi un'irriconoscibile, inconoscibile
e vaga): mi sono messo presto, allora, in cuore (mediante gli occhi, canonicamente),
un dittico di gambe alternative (e interminate, cupe, inattingibili): ma mi commosse
(un niente, e mi piangevo), riagganciandomi sola, me tutto solo, sopra una rampa
di solinghe scale:

me la sono giocata, finalmente (me la sono sprecata), per una monacense
smonacata (che era, a suo modo, pure, una Delikatesse delicata, cooperante e, forse,
perficiente): (e ho colto l'occasione, in ogni caso, di sottrarla, con torta al cioccolato,
a un moscardino di un francesino):

quando scoppiò lo strazio degli adieux, le venni meno,
tra le mani, almeno, a quella illuminante illuminata, nel giro di un incongruo
zufrieden sehr, e un non so che di un non so quale ich weiss nicht, così,
nel rotolio di un balbettìo:

(la grazia, quando arriva, mi è eccessiva):

XI

the most gracious of graces (and the most efficacious) is the girl who picks me up in Tegel,
crouched in ambush, to load me up onto a jeep, to unload me at a Hilton
(Kroneflügel): then I missed her on the phone (and at that Empfang, there at the Beethoven-Saal,
along with the burgomaster's speech, I found her almost unrecognisable, unknowable
and hazy): immediately I put into my heart (through my eyes, as is truly right and proper),
a diptych of other legs (interminable, mysterious, unattainable): but she moved me
and I was crying, nearly, picking me up again on her own, me all alone on a flight
of lonesome stairs:

       in the end I gambled her away (I wasted her) for an un-Munichy
Municher (who was, in her way, however, a delicate Delikatesse, cooperative and, maybe,
improving): (and I seized the occasion, in any case, to rescue her, with chocolate cake,
from a foppish little frenchman):

       when the heartbreak of our adieux happened, I swooned on her,
in her hands, at least, that luminous illuminata, in the course of an incongruous
zufrieden sehr, and I don't know which of an I don't know what type of ich weiss nicht, thus,
in the roll of a stammer:

       (grace, when it comes, just overwhelms me):

XII

ho penetrato (si fa per dire, ma si fa pure per fare) tutti i nomi santi (che sono
tanti, e sono molto multipli):

che è sorto (è ovvio, è troppo ovvio, è proprio vero), presso Cafàrnao (o come diavolo
si può scrivere e pronunciare), tra archeologie sacre e profane (VIA MARIS, MILESTONE,
come grida un grosso cippo, graffiato dai graffiti, cubitalmente e crudelmente), over
the house of St. Peter:

            menziono a caso, qui, per te, un St. Peter Memorial,

            e io mi dibattevo in una banda gigante di gitanti (non esclusa
la minima argentina signorina), tra gli spari di mille ladies and gentlemen, gratis
forniti dalla grulla guida: (e aggiungi, ma in versione palestinese, un pesce sampietrino,
che fu magistralmente degustato, con un docente pisano e altra gente, sulla spiaggia
di Tiberiade, prima del giro in battello, quando esplosivo eruppe, da un tango fragoroso,
un pot-pourri inesauribile):

XII

I penetrated (so to speak, so too indeed to act) all the holy names (which are
many and are very various):

      I mention, at random, here, for you, a St. Peter Memorial,
which has sprung up (that's obvious, too obviously, absolutely certainly), near Capernaum (oh how
the devil
do you write and pronounce that), amid sacred and profane ruins (VIA MARIS, MILESTONE,
as a great slab yells, disfigured by graffiti, proclaims, in large and cruel lettering), over
the house of St. Peter:

      and I floundered in the midst of a huge troupe of tourists (including
the littlest Argentinian woman), listening to 1,000 screeches of ladies and gentlemen provided, gratis,
by the silly guide: (and I add, but in the Palestinian version, a St. Peter fish,
which was dexterously consumed, in the company of a Pisan teacher and sundry others, on the shore
of Tiberias, just before the boattrip, where there erupted explosively, from a turbulent tango,
an inexhaustible pot-pourri):

poi, di fronte al capriccio di un Caprice (che è una gallery
che è una jewellery, una diamond factory, con cinesalà didattica), il casino di un rimborso
improbabile di V.A.T. (o T.V.A.), facendomi incazzare, ti ha privato di due perle: erano
le tue pietre zodiacali, che significano "health, wealth and long life" (l'oroscopo
non muta), con lo sconto di un 15%:

quanto a penetrazioni, tuttavia, fu al tempio
di Afrodite di Adriano (impropriamente additato, oggimai, come un sepolcro santo),
che ho immesso avidamente la mia mano, tremula e ignuda, strisciandomi, ricurvo tanatofilo,
sotto un altare raro, dentro il piccolo abisso congelato di quella vulva della verità:

then, opposite a capricious place called Caprice (which is an arcade
which is a jewellery, a diamond factory with its own explanatory cinema), the mess
of the V.A.T. (or T.V.A.), unlikely to be recovered,making me irritated, deprived you of two pearls:
namely
your zodiacstones, signifying "health, wealth and long life" (the horoscope
doesn't change), with a discount of 15%:

as for penetration, however, it was at the temple
of Hadrian's Aphrodite (improperly presented, nowadays, as a holy sepulchre),
that I eagerly shoved my hand, naked and trembling, a furtive, stooping thanatophile,
beneath a rare altarstone, into the small frozen abyss of that vulva of truth:

ci ha messo molta sua delicatezza, pur di tenermela un po' a bada, il savio Natan
(e finalmente per discacciarmela via), quell'angelica Ofelia indemoniata (la rediviva
Corinna, la posseduta dal K.G.B., ma già in procinto di emigrare a Hollywood, dove deve
rivendicarsi una sceneggiatura, di cui fu iniquamente depredata):

e io

— io stavo come inchiodato a un'enigmatica littera Pythagorae: (in vertigine vera, ero
un pidocchio, tra i suoi riccioli imbrillantati, disposto già, per ritrovarmi, a perdermi):
e lei

— lei improvvisava quartine di calligrammi, lì su due piedi, a bassa voce, spirando
spiritosi spiritelli, polputi ma impalpabili, follemente sciamanti a schiere, a squadrati
squadroni, spremuti a forza fuori dalle sue pure pupille di perversa:

ma, avendo avuto, già,

da tremare abbastanza, e da lasciarci intiera la mia testa, per il fulgore vago
di una Giuditta devastante tanto, ho liquidato tutta la baracca, abbandonandomi,
esausto, alla piatta perfidia di un'estremorientale Salomè (bella come un'aurora
che tramonta lungo la Via Dolorosa, all'altezza della stazione settima, più o meno):
mi barattò due baci, uno per guancia (uno così di qua, uno cosà di là), per pura carità,
per un biglietto verde, da due dollari:

(quanto valesse non so, ma è rarissimo):

XIII

Nathan the wise has used great delicacy to keep her somewhat at bay from me
(and finally to hunt her away from me), that angelic demoniac Ophelia (that reborn
Corinna, that possessed one from the K.G.B., but already on the point of emigrating to Hollywood where
she has to

retrieve a script she was maliciously deprived of):

                                                    and I

— I was like someone nailed to an enigmatic Pythagorean letter: (in absolute giddiness, I was
a louse moving through her brillantined curls, disposed already to lose myself to find myself):
and she

              —she was improvising quatrains of calligrams, there on two feet, in a low voice, breathing out
spirited little spirits, fleshy but impalpable, swarming crazily in crowds, in squared
squadrons, squeezed forcedly out through her pure and perverse eyes:

                                                    but having had already
enough of being shaken, and of being driven out of my mind, through the hazy lightning flash
of such a devastating Judith, I wiped out the whole shebang, abandoning myself,
exhausted, to the flat perfidy of a fareastern Salome (lovely as a dawn
which goes down along the Via Dolorosa at the level, more or less, of the seventh station):
she bartered me two kisses, one on the cheek (one like this, here, one like that, there), out of sheer charity,
for a green two dollar bill:

              (what 'twas worth I don't know, but it's most rare):

XIV

rimasero assolutamente esterrefatti, e non privi d'invidia, i tre macedoni, allorquando, in casa di Yehuda, quella fotografa (l'additerò così, qui, per intenderci, adesso), tutta verso di me molto protesa, sporgendosi a sguardarmi, loquacissima, dalle ginocchia del marito assiso (un grande costruttore, mi hanno detto), manifestò la sua predilezione e inclinazione, senza riserve, la prima sera, psicoposizionalmente, nei miei confronti: (e ne giunse notizia, come un fulmine, in Almería e in Ginevra):

e:

quella è molto aggressiva, mi dicevano, deglutendo cognac, e molto ardente: (e invano io rilevavo e ribadivo, difendendomi a stento, che ero un vecchio vecchissimo, e anzi un quasi agonizzante): (e buono, al massimo, per un minimo flirt):

l'ho ritrovata,

due giorni dopo, insperata, all'altezza del cardo, nel casino della casbah: (e avevo, certo, nel momento che mi abbracciava stretto, gli occhi da pesce lesso entusiasmato): (alla Gabin le Moko, uso anni Trenta):

mancava tutto il resto: salvo che, quella Gaby

anni Novanta, lunedì notte, al nostro appuntamento, non si fece vedere, puntualissima:

they were absolutely amazed, and maybe a little jealous, those three Macedonians, when, in Yehuda's house, that photographer (I will describe her thus, here, for clarity, for the present), wholly stretched out towards me, leaning to look at me, full of talk, from the knees of her seated husband (a bigtime builder, they said), on that first evening, showed, her predilection and inclination, without reserve, the first evening, psychopositionally, towards me: (and the news travelled like lightning to Almeria and Geneva):
and:

    that lassie is very forward, they said, slurping cognac, and very passionate: (and uselessly I pointed out and stressed, in my feeble defence, that I was old and very old, and better still almost at death's door): (and good enough, at best, for a minimal flirtation):

    I found her again, two days later, unhoped-for, level with the thistle, in the confusion of the casbah: (and surely just as she was squeezing me tightly, my eyes shone like those of an ecstatic boiled fish): (like Gabin le Moko, in thirties style):

    everyone else was missing: except, Monday night, that Gaby of the Nineties didn't show up, for our appointment, most punctually:

XV

ma come siamo, poi, noi (gli italiani)?

       la questione fu presa di petto, e strenuamente
sviscerata, una sera, a una cena, al Montefiore del Mishkenot, con alcuni opulenti
semibulgari (e con una semibulgaressa, o bulgaressa proprio, solidissima):

                                             (es.:

siamo sensuali? sessuali? sensibili?): (siamo sessuatamente sensati?): (sensatamente
sessuati?): (tutto dipende, alla fine, dalla lingua che ti sei scelto): (dalla lingua
che ti sei subito, soprattutto): (e qui, come da tanti squisiti fumi passivi, sei stato
violentato da scariche di implacabili fotografie (e di implacabili lingue) passive):
(e la lingua passiva, lo vedi, anzi lo senti (sensibilmente lo senti, se lo senti):
(se la senti): la lingua è già, da sola, un'ansiogena anfibologia: sessualmente
sensata, per l'appunto):

           tale mi fu l'ultima sera, che mi fu l'ultima cena, e che fu,
come da programma, intiera, un sexy-booze and -schmooze:

                                      (gaio usque ad mortem):

so what are we like then, we (Italians?)

the question was met head on, and strenuously
dissected, one evening, at a meal, in the Montefiore in Mishkenot, in the company of some opulent
half-bulgarians (and one half-bulgaress, or fullbred bulgaress, mightily hefty):

(e.g.:

are we sensual? sexual? sensitive?): (are we sexually sensate?): (sensately
sexual?): (it all depends, in the end, on the language you've chosen): (on the language
above all, you've been subjected to): (and here, as from so many exquisite passive fumes, you've been
ravished by myriads of implacable, passive photographs (and so many implacable tongues)):
and this passive tongue, don't you see, or sense, rather (you sense it sensorially, if you sense it):
(if you sense the tongue): the tongue already, in itself, is an anxiolytic amphibology: sexually
sensate, which is the whole point):

such was my last evening, my last supper, and it was,
as planned, a complete sexy-booze and -schmooze:

(cheerful usque ad mortem):

XVI

sono 613, mi pare, i veri comandamenti: (e un vero scherzo è il decalogo,
al confronto): molti sono però gli impraticati, in quanto impraticabili, da troppo
tempo (e forse per sempre):

              me lo ha spiegato Davide, il dragomanno (come si legge a stampa,
sulla sua carta da visita), quando, nel limbo del quartiere armeno, crepitò, per annuncio
del rito, surrogando le campane, la lignea percussione fragorosa, secondo tradizione,
del meraviglioso seminarista malinconico:

                              (e uscimmo dalla porta del letame):

XVI

there are, I fancy, 613 real commandments: (and the decalogue is a real doddle
in comparison): but many of them haven't been observed, inasmuch as they can't be observed, for too long
a time (since the beginning perhaps):

> David, the dragoman (as you can read it printed,
> on his visiting card), explained all that, when, in the limbo of the Armenian quarter, there broke out,
> to announce
> the service, replacing the bells, the traditionally loud, wooden percussion
> of the marvellous, melancholy seminarian:

> > (and we left by the Gate of Excrement):

XVII

me li sono pensati, i tuoi settanta, settanta volte sette, nel derelitto stabilimento
balneare di quello pseudomare, mortalmente depresso (e depressivo), quando (puntando
verso le cave più scavate dei relitti dei rotoli), con Yizhak (a noi liofilizzati, benché
ubriacati da molte minerali gasatissime), ci fiorì, repentina, dall'autoradio clamorosa,
clamorosamente straziata e straniata, tutta una Casta Diva disperata:

                                                                    idem, ancora,

quando, sopra le rive del Giordano, incrociandomi un'anabattista anadiomene (che mi stava
velata, fasciata, la sindone incollata lì al suo nudo), ho scoperto l'hamsah, nell'edicola
del bazar:

        e allora, come si dice un qualunque happy birthday, io ti dissi, Luciano,
da lontano, un largo e lungo good luck (and look), spalancandomi gli occhi delle mani:

XVII

I thought of your seventy, seventy times seven, in the derelict bathing
establishment of that pseudo-beach, fatal depression (and depressing), when (headed
towards the most excavated of the caves of the remains of the scrolls), with Yizhak (lyophilised, al-
though

we were drunk on so many overgassy minerals), there rose, unexpectedly, from the blaring car-radio,
blaringly anguished and alien, the whole of a desperate Casta Diva:

                         idem, once more,

when, on the banks of the Jordan, coming across her, that anadiomine anabaptist (who was veiled,
swathed, the shroud pulled tightly round her nakedness), I discovered the hamsah, in the bazaar
bookstall:

      and then, as one says any sort of a happy birthday, I wished you, Luciano,
from afar, a great and prolonged good luck (and look), opening wide the eyes of my hands;